The TRUTH ABOUT FAIRIES

PICTURE WINDOW BOOKS
a capstone imprint

BY J. ANGELIQUE JOHNSON ILLUSTRATED BY CAROLINA FARIAS

For Brynja and Leif

Thanks to our advisers for their expertise, research, and advice:

Elizabeth Tucker, Ph.D., Professor of English
Binghamton University, Binghamton, New York

Terry Flaherty, Ph.D., Professor of English
Minnesota State University, Mankato

Editors: Shelly Lyons and Jennifer Besel
Designer: Lori Bye
Art Director: Nathan Gassman
Production Specialist: Jane Klenk
The illustrations in this book were created with acrylics and watercolor.

Picture Window Books
151 Good Counsel Drive
P.O. Box 669
Mankato, MN 56002-0669
877-845-8392
www.capstonepub.com

Printed in the United States of America in North Mankato, Minnesota.
052010
005813R

All books published by Picture Window Books
are manufactured with paper containing at least
10 percent post-consumer waste.

Library of Congress Cataloging-in-Publication Data
Johnson, J. Angelique.
The truth about fairies / written by J. Angelique Johnson ;
illustrated by Carolina Farias.
p. cm. — (Fairy-tale superstars)
Includes index.
ISBN 978-1-4048-5746-9 (library binding)
1. Fairies—Juvenile fiction. I. Farías, Carolina, ill. II. Title.
GR549.L47 2010
398.21—dc22   2009030073

Are Fairies Real?

Fairies seem to twinkle and shine. But are fairies real? Of course not! Fairies are make-believe creatures that have sprinkled magic through stories for hundreds of years.

Fairy History

Fairies flutter through stories all around the world. Some stories say a fairy is born from a baby's first laugh. Other legends say fairies were once angels.

People created stories about fairies to explain things they didn't understand. Some people in England blamed fairies for bad crops. In Ireland, people said fairies soured milk.

What Do Fairies Look Like?

Fairies can look like almost anything. Some have pointy noses and crooked teeth. Some even look like animals with wings.

Some well-known fairies look like tiny princesses and princes. They have silvery wings. They twinkle like stars.

pointy nose

large ears

tiny body

clothing made of leaves

silvery wings

flower petal clothing

Fairies wear special clothing. A fairy's shirt might be made of spiders' webs or leaves. A fairy's dress can be made from flower petals.

One storybook fairy wore tights made out of an apple core. His slippers were made from the skin of a mouse.

Where Do Fairies Live?

Fairies live in the Fairy Realm. The Fairy Realm is a make-believe place that people can't see.

A Welsh myth says the Fairy Realm can be seen only from inside a circle of wild mushrooms. But watch out! People who step into the Fairy Realm rarely come back.

Curious fairies travel outside the Fairy Realm.
These fairies play in gardens and birds' nests.
They nap in empty nutshells.

In some stories, fairies leave the Fairy Realm to help people in need. The Blue Fairy in Carlo Collodi's famous story, *The Adventures of Pinocchio*, even helps a puppet. The Blue Fairy teaches a puppet how to behave well. Then she turns him into a real boy.

Fairy Behavior

Fairies can be good or bad. Most are a bit of both. They like to punish people who do bad things. In one story, fairies punished a lazy woman. They pinched her arms and legs. Another fairy rewarded a polite man with gold.

Storybook fairies are full of tricks. A fairy might pretend to be a songbird. It would sing a beautiful girl to sleep.

Another fairy might steal a baby from its crib. In its place, the fairy would leave a skinny, wrinkled fairy.

Many fairies are quick to get angry. In an Irish tale, a young boy named Jack hears fairies singing. Jack interrupts the fairies' song with his own terrible singing. The fairies cast an evil spell on Jack. They leave him with two humps on his back!

Fairies also do mean things when they are jealous. The most famous fairy is Tinker Bell from J. M. Barrie's story, *Peter Pan*. Tinker Bell becomes jealous of a human girl. She talks some boys into shooting arrows at the girl. Luckily they miss!

Fairy Magic

Fairies are magical. They use magic to fool people into seeing things that aren't real. A dark cave might look like a beautiful room. An ugly fairy might look like a handsome boy. This magic is called fairy glamour.

Fairy godmothers use magic to help their godchildren. Cinderella's fairy godmother helped her go to a ball.

In *Sleeping Beauty*, Aurora's fairy godmothers used magic to keep her safe from an evil fairy.

Fairies Today

Fairies are still popular today. Some people paint pictures of glittering fairies. Other people write stories about fairies that hide among us. Movies show us all kinds of fairies.

Fairies are not real. But these magical creatures are fun to imagine. Wouldn't you agree?

Fun Facts About Fairies

Never eat fairy food! It is filled with magic that makes people forget everything they know.

The best time to see a fairy is when the sun is setting.

A four-leaf clover lets people see past fairy glamour.

Fairies don't like salt, iron, or stinky herbs like garlic.

A fit of laughter might mean a fairy is nearby.

Glossary

fairy glamour—magic used by fairies to change what people see

Fairy Realm—a make-believe place where fairies live

imagine—to picture something in your mind

jealous—when a person wants something another person has, like money or fame

legend—a story handed down from earlier times

myth—a make-believe story

popular—liked by many

punish—to make a person suffer for behaving badly

reward—something done or given to show thanks

Index

To Learn More

More Books to Read

Burns, Jan. *Fairies*. Detroit: KidHaven Press, 2007.

Piumini, Roberto. *Cinderella*. Minneapolis: Picture Window Books, 2010.

Werner, Jane, ed. *The Giant Golden Book of Elves and Fairies*. New York: Golden Books, 2008.

Zamorsky, Tania. *Peter Pan: Retold from the J.M. Barrie Original*. New York: Sterling, 2009.

Internet Sites

FactHound offers a safe, fun way to find Internet sites related to this book. All of the sites on FactHound have been researched by our staff.

Here's all you do:

Visit *www.facthound.com*

FactHound will fetch the best sites for you!

Look for all the books in the Fairy-Tale Superstars series:

The Truth About Dragons
The Truth About Fairies

The Truth About Princesses
The Truth About Trolls